THE WHISPERING TREE
poems of love and longing

Satchidanandan is an important global poet. He distils and expresses humanity in a voice that is at once local and universal, individual and everyman's. He is also a major English-language poet, due to the sterling quality of his self-translations from the original Malayalam. His poems are of perennial import; they sustain the spirit, speaking with equal eloquence to the mind and the heart.

Philip Nikolayev | American poet and editor, *Fulcrum* on *The Missing Rib*

Satchidanandan's poetry is a lyre with many chords: it may seem light with joking tunes, it can be harsh and nearly cruel: sometimes it seems to unite all these characteristics together, especially when his poems have the form of a dialogue.

Antonio Menniti Ipplito | Italian critic, speech introducing his Italian collection, *I Riti Della Terra*

In Satchidanandan, one notices a great modernity, a chosen but simple terminology of immediate understanding, something like a non-rhetorical dialogue with himself and with the reader, a wealth of symbology, a fascinating smoothness of the verses, a subtle irony.

Carlo Savini | Italian Critic, introduction to *I Rit ella Terra*

These are poems of great strength and power, a moving tribute to the generation in which we live.

Jayanta Mahapatra | on the poems in *Summer Rain*

His poetry attests to the abiding concern of the poet for all mankind. Synthesising hope with despair, the poet always expects light at the end of the tunnel.

The Asian Age | on *Summer Rain*

His words shock us, make us look inward, introspect and search for the ultimate truth.

Observer | on *Summer Rain*

This book is a marvel, a lifting of a great weight of treasure into the Irish language.

Caitriona Ni Cheirichin | on his selected poems in Irish, *Rogha Danta* translated by Gabriel Rosenstock

Photo credit: Sikha Khanna

THE WHISPERING TREE
poems of love and longing

K. Satchidanandan

[translated from Malayalam by the poet]

CLASSIX

CLASSIX

Published by CLASSIX (a *Hawakal* imprint)
33/1/2, K B Sarani, Mall Road, Kolkata 700080, India

info@hawakal.com
www.hawakal.com

First edition June 2020

Cover image: Shutterstock
Cover design: Bitan Chakraborty

Typeset in Baskerville (11 pts) & Tarjan Pro (13 pts)
Printed & bound in Thomson Press (India) Ltd, New Delhi 110020

ISBN : 978-81-945273-5-0

Price: 450 INR | USD 15.99

CONTENTS

A SMALL SPRING

A small spring,
That a casket can contain,
Or the pupil of an eye.

So intense were its
Colours and odours
It couldn't have lasted long—
Like some adolescent loves.

A small spring,
Like a Flame of the Forest
In full bloom unaware of
The arrival of winter.

Why did it vanish so fast,
I asked the wind
A drizzle was the reply.
It had some floating petals
That God had kept as bookmarks
In Life's account book.
I could not decipher the script
As they were dried up, wrinkled.

A small spring,
More scorching than summer,

Burning with pleasure.
I stopped kissing anyone
Except solitude in her
Tight black gown.

I open the windows wide:
Suppose it comes back like
The spilt wine returning to the cup
Shouting with passion,
'Come and lift me up!'

A small spring, a pang,
My lips quiver with desire
Cheers!

—
2020

AFTER WE PARTED

Every day after we parted
I have been struggling to recreate you
out of my memory, cell by cell
quietly sitting in the dim,
cold winter evenings.

I pierce my tongue
with my father's trident
to convince myself
that I have not lost you.
And when, instead of words,
blood fills my mouth,
I taste your lips.
I sit in meditation
filling my ears with molten bronze
so that the world's noises may
cease one by one until
only your anklet-like laughter remains.

I place a huge stone on my chest.
Slowly your beloved face
and your straight hairs,
tempters to my fingers,
begin to appear out of the mist.
I break my right arm,

twisting and turning it
between the window bars.
Your sobbing arms reach out
to hold me in a tight hug.
I pour acid into my eyes.
Your glowing breasts
invite my thirsty tongue.
I bury my hip in sacrificial fire,
your wetness fuels the embers.

This is love:
Head down I need to hang
and burn out inch by inch
so that I may give you form.

The second spring of desire
blooms from the burning pain
of the body parting has maimed.
When love is free of flesh
kisses turn orphans.
Only words remain, and dreams
looking for space to express themselves
in the choking wilderness:
Madanan, Divakaran,*
naked, erect.

—

2005

*Love-lorn protagonists in Kumaran Asan's verse narratives

AGAIN

1

I took one step forward,
left behind fifty summers.
You extended an arm,
walked fifty springs backward.
Together we built a home
for the hugs we had not exchanged.
All the missing birds
flew in there to nest.
All the rains
that had not drenched us
turned into folksongs
and flooded our courtyard.
We made a garden
for the homeless kisses.
All the fifty winters
of our separation
grew fragrant in a second.
We grew wings.

2

Do trees grow in deserts?
Yes, those Trees of Life
will have the spirits of rainbows.

3

In those years of absence
we traversed known darkness
and unknown stars.
On the crocodile skin of drudgery
we wrote 'silk'
with blood from our wounds.

Like a man hurriedly turning the pages
of the survivors' list after an accident
to find one's mate
I sought you in every woman
I came across.
I stayed for a while
on names that sounded similar.
Like a woman, wreath in hand,
reading with trembling lips
the names engraved
on the soldiers' tombs after the war
you too must have
looked for me
among the men you met.

4

We were racing faster than time
and yet we stood where we had been
like in dreams: on the two sides
of the wall of mist and pollen...
Our screams were voiceless, anguished,
like those of the people
silently running away from poison gas
holding their lives on their palms.
Our life was the untasted wine
spilled from broken bottles.

5

We saw each other when
the mist and pollen settled.
In that shock of recognition
everything came back
like memories to an amnesiac:
the first encounter,
the first love-poem.
You were a child
lean like paddy, and I, a boy
shy like a hanging hibiscus.

They are no more.
A mature woman
and a weary old man
now live in two worlds
holding them in their memory.

6

My blood still carries your name
to every one of my parts.
Where had our love
gone into hiding
all these years? In which
planet's unfamiliar waters? In which
star's freezing night?

Eight demons call out your name
from eight directions.
Love, light, rise, rise
from prisoners' drums!

7

We are the remains of
an ancient civilization,
to land up soon in God's museum.

8

I know, we are extending our hands
from sinking ships: between us
is a wide-open blue jaw.
We keep falling into it,
our hands still in each other's,
our nostrils throbbing
to catch the scent of
the other world's flowers,
our lips humming the tune
of the song whose words we lost
among our worldly chores,
lending to the freezing water
the warmth of our desire,
letting the gold fish
swim about our sinking heads,
opening one water-lily
for each rung of the liquid ladder,
until our entwined feet
touch the corals on the seabed.

It is not too late still.
There is an Ashoka tree
Still awaiting you in my Lanka,
The very last shade
no messenger can
ever hope to reach.

—
2014

BURNT POEMS

I am a half-burnt poem.
Yes, you guessed right,
a girl's love poem.

Girls' love poems have
Seldom escaped fire:
father's fire, brother's fire,
even mother's, an heirloom.

Only some girls half-escape:
those half-charred ones
we call Sylvia Plath,
Anna Akhmatova
or Kamala Das.

Some girls, to escape fire,
hide their desire
under the veil of piety:
thus is born a Meera,
an Andal, a Mahadevi Akka.

Every nun is a burnt
love-poem, addressed to
the ever-young Jesus.

Rarely, very rarely,
one girl learns to
laugh at the world
with that tender affection
only women are capable of.
Then the world names her
Wislawa Szymborska.

Of course, Sappho:
she was saved only as
her love poems were
addressed to women.

—

2012

FIRST LOVE

The first love is like the first rabbit:
a feather-soft wonder leaping up
on the dew-drenched green with
ruby-eyes and ears of pearl...

Taming it is not easy:
It flees into hiding before
you stretch your hands.
Barking basic instincts scare it away.
A murmuring leaf even
can stun it into silence,
and a fragrant rose burn its nose.

In the end we manage to catch hold of it
dazzling its eyes with intense passion
place it on our laps
and begin fondling it,
and soon it melts down like snow.

Only a white light throbs where it was
and a single snow-flake is left behind:
a frozen tear-drop.

—

1994

HELPLESS

I pour water on you taking care
so that not one leaf
of your hair gets wet,
not one bud falls off your body,
imagining that the bathroom in the city
is the village-well's rim overgrown with
green algae, fungi and ferns.

Then I summon sandalwood and rural herbs
to memory and bent as in prayer,
I soap your idol.
First, your feet, gently,
as if they were clouds
that would rain at a touch.
Like sunbeams falling
at a slant on the sky
the tender light of the soap's foam
renders your soles transparent.
My fingers slide between your toes
gently plucking the red grapes
I see ripening there.
When I polish your nails,
I am a careful sculptor working on ivory.
Then I press your calves until
they leap up like rabbits that fancy
tender grass growing on the wet floor.

In the next phase of my worship
all atremble with love, or may be, devotion
I stand up, bow and engrave your thighs
with my hands full of foam.
My hands slip, like falling from
bed in a dream, and move, trembling,
to your hips, your navel,
to the alphabet-like curves of your belly,
upwards as if reminded of something,
to the bouquets of your breasts
swaying in the wind,
to their diamond crowns.

I wash and clean your neck's lane
along which love's spring descends
from your head to your body.
Then your flag, your face,
too glowing to be polished.
I cover it yet with the little rainbows
in the bubbles, burnish the cheeks
as a Kathakali dancer does with orpiment,
turn your lips into dawns.
eyelids into petals, forehead into moonlight.

Now let loose your hair, like the day
loosening the night; let me wash
each fragrant strand of darkness
one by one until they return to
their own scent feasting on oil,
to that mixed heady fragrance,
of the breeze that carries the smells
of blue berry, sandalwood and vetiver.
Now I will turn you into a mermaid,
a shape-shifting liquid virgin.

Now it is your turn.
You may have to use the lexicons
of many languages to turn me into Apollo,
rub and wash me with stone and glass.
But with a single look you transform me
into Michelangelo's David.
Your soft touch makes me
the broad-chested Gotama
of your drawing room, the prince
before he became the Buddha.

I forget my impoverished childhood
and become a handsome demon,
a *gandharva* in your moist hands.
I hide the devil within me.
My body sings as you play me like a *veena,*
every cell sings; I dwindle, melt.

Now there is neither me nor you.
Water, endless water, and a blue lotus
made of two bodies stuck together.

—

2018

HOW LOVE DIES THESE DAYS

Love dies as crows do:
we just don't realize
when one day we
cease to see one.

That name that had once
sweetened your body and soul
doesn't even get time
enough to turn bitter.
All those pet names we had given her
vanish from the dictionary.
Even the computer forgets
the false usernames and passwords
we had created to write to her.
Messages go out as their
electric supply gets cut.
Her facebook page you used to
visit thrice a day is
now the remotest star.
The voice that had
quickened your heart beat
is a song you had once heard
in a passing vehicle,
her odour is a nameless flower
you had seen in a flash

on a hill in childhood,
her touch, that of a wayside tree
rubbing against your cloth.

You have learnt that letter too.
Now that name will dissolve
in the rainwater and
join the ocean of names,
glistening on the edge of waves
on certain crazy afternoons,
like a knife's edge in the sunlight.

—
2013

IMPERFECT

'Imperfect is the summit' – Yves Bonnefoy

1
PRESENCE
(Stockholm, October 3-21, 1997)

From where did you come
from where did I come
from where did we come, my love,
in this garden of yellow maple leaves
in this evening that sticks to our feet
in this rain bursting forth
from a bygone age
in this chill that preceded the stars?
From the roots of tangled lanes
or the dumb night before creation
from the sea still dreaming of shells
or the word-like throb of life
first heard from a glacier?
Was it lightning that carried you here or
the white stone's longing for heaven?

You caress my tired limbs like a wave;
Salt sticks to my cheeks.
Are you a woman or an inland sea?
You turn into water between my fingers
A dance beyond life and death

leads us out of Time.
We leave earth for another moonlight
Our language is no more human;
it is of the birds bathed in sunlight,
of the collyrium and the spring shower,
of elves, perhaps.

(August Strindberg Park)

2

You are a waterfall
descending the stairs.
I am a grey rock below
eager for your arrival.
Dance over me, tickle me into life,
cover me with green.
Gush forth, let fish swim
on my head faster than eyes
Let the weightless shadow
of a rainbow fall
on my ancient back, and
a lily-like heart grow within.

You had descended the stairs of Time
Now we are in earth's childhood.

(Hotel Strindbeg)

3

Infinity's longing we name sea,
then translate it into cloud and rain,
islands and seconds.
Waves twitter like endless birds
waking up the sun as we float
amidst a thousand islets.
October wind turns us into
a pair of trembling bluebells.
Shorn of our crown of thorns
We swing weightless on a creeper,
Petal to petal.
We have given the sea
everything we had:
our memory, our faith,
our shame, our high tide,
as if to the graveyard.

No more do we fear life.
Wave, carry us to the beginning
of sunbeams and longings,
to the fiesta of flags and lights.

(In a ship on the Archepelago)

4

White wine foams up like Spring,
but the wings it gave us could not
lift us even up to pain.
No one becomes a sunflower by
meditating on it.
We shun everything that is
harsh and intense, like truth.
We are no sky; we are humans, finite.
The more we try to forget it
the more real we become.
Your insensitivity makes you sob
until all stars turn black.

These shoulders scarred by
fifty years on earth could
hardly be a refuge to their own head.
Yet, rest your fragrant head on them
as on the wall of a prison-cell
and feel as secure as a wingless bird
in a tree's hollow in a forest on fire.

(Rydborg Restaurant)

5

You draw me into you
Like the sun the lake
Until I turn inside out
And reveal my floor.
Then I fall
My body is rain,
through which you glisten.
Green things are born
wherever I fall until
the woods grow dense.
You shine through them too
till I become a river
and your lips drink me again.

(*At writer Louisa's home on the banks of a lake*)

6

The train takes us along countrysides
autumn has painted yellow.
You listen to my poems
as we sit huddled together
like twins in the train's warm womb,
distances dangling from its claws.
I fill you like wind sneaking in
through the keyhole.
Fullness is not for us; our words
lost their wings long ago.
They limp, stammer, as they
try to sing: not a letter comes out.
I run my fingers over your ears
as if they were words,
as if this were you.
No, this is not you; you are elsewhere:
this unreal image will do for me.
Reality is not in my grip;
illusions I can access
through my stammer,
touch with my trembling lips.

Poetry is a river with
no more bridges, but only their images.

(Going to Uppsala by train)

7

Theatre is not illusion's bubble...
The destiny of an insane patriarch
rants and raves on the stage.
We too are climbing
with our unseen crosses
and burning bodies
towards a death that is
neither sacrifice nor suicide.

The thirsty dead drink our thirst
to grow blood and muscles.
It is they that besiege us,
they who cry, 'love me, love me.'
not me nor you.
Love me still, snap the noose
in which I twist and turn,
lay me in life's tender lap
with my bleeding stigmata
as in the Mother's lap.

(Watching Strindberg's play, 'Father')

8

Your gaze is stone, it
breaks me like glass.
What are you yearning for: wine,
or love that pollinates the vineyards?
I can touch your intoxication with mine.
Only a thin veil divides joy and us—
Is it the forgetting of our last life
or the fear of the next?
Now we are in a world where
sin is mixed with joy
like poison with nectar.
The ecstasy of the unwise
leads us to the wisdom of the separated.
Fire is not only in the wine,
it is in silence and in flower,
in words and in water,
on the tongue and the navel.
Hold me tight, like death,
Bite me, Goddess of Venom,
turn me blue
like this blue-black sky.

(At cocktails at the Writers' Union)

9

This Noah brought seeds
from the far corners of the earth
to cultivate this garden of signs.
He didn't know plants have another hell.
In the painful effort to fly
they grow branches, their bodies
bend and twist as they strain to speak.
Shoots burst forth at last instead of words.
Flowers are wounds.
Leaves shake off their green
and, tired of ther leaf's life, fall.
He never understood plants:
their hearts brim with love.
Love cannot stand
definitions an categories.
It simply grows where there is
some water, some light.
I won't count your leaves
nor do I need to know
the shapes and shades of your petals.
Just wind round me,
Fill me with your scents
so that this driftwood that
fought every stone for a handful of flowers
may dream up new shoots.
And time may turn into a sweet seed
traveling through it
to the joys of the fruit.

(*In the Garden of Linnaeus, Uppsala*)

10

These emerald hills are
the graveyards of ancient seamen.
Oceans were puddles to their vessels,
at times their graves.
Swaying in waves and winds,
they touched new lands
like words landing in poems,
suddenly, unforeseen.

We too are a pair of words
in search of our poem.
Someone uttered us,
somcone sculpted us into form.
Some consecrate us in lines.
We weep with other words at times,
at times laugh or pray.
Some befriend us, some own.
Contexts lend us meaning.
We roll on tongues, salty, sour, hot,
like another tongue in kiss.
We break the bars, the lines,
and stealthily leave the pages,
to be caught once again,
again to scale the wall.
We are the realisation
deferred eternally, expression
ever incomplete,
unattainable climax.

(Viking Mounts, Uppsala)

11

I write your name
on the morning snow,
on every object where once
the poet wrote liberty's name.*
I need not wipe off that name
To write yours; there is
space enough for love
on earth and sky.
I sleep on the bed of your names,
I wake up into the twittering of your names.
Your name appears wherever I touch:
on the brown of the fallen leaves,
on the dark walls of primal caves,
on the butcher's door,
on wet paint, wet blood,
on the ploughed field,
on the butterfly wings of moonlight,
in coffee, in salt,
on the horse's hooves, the dancer's gestures,
on the shoulders of stars,
in honey, in venom, on waves, sand, roots,
on the axe, on bullets,
on the hangman's rope,
on the cold floor of the mortuary,
on the soft back of the tombstone.

(*Cold morning, walking*)

12

We, two kids, play mother and father.
We do not know the meaning
of embrace, the electricity of kiss.
Yet we touch some leaves,
some flowers, fruits even.
Nature watches us with affection:
this brief flaming up of the longing
to perpetuate, this basic instinct
he filled beings with,
this vain survival gesture.
Listen to the night
scampering along the corridor.

13

That we should part bfore
our names on the snow vanish!
Let me play you like a tambourine
until you melt into strains.
Let us keep flying all night.
We are riding a cloud all our own;
at the end of the joy-ride,
a sharp day awaits us.
How I loathe the sun,
that reminder of evanescence!

What was illusion, what is real,
I do not wish to know.
That which is beyond words
is without grammar.
That which has not begun
does not end too.

(*On the flight back*)

2
ABSENCE
(Delhi, Oct.22-Nov.10; Paris, Nov.11-23)

14

Each presence has a shade
sheltering me from the rain of memories.

You are formles now,
a voice carried by waves
from beyond the mountains,
a laugh, a sigh, a kiss with silver wings.

Waterfalls cannot laugh like you,
peepals cannot chatter, drizzles cajole
nor dawns kiss, like you.

Poets can embrace mere voice,
possess, to love, to enter.
Thus I enter you, all awake,
my senses at one point,
like a ghost making itself
visible to the living
until I barter my winter
for your spring.

15

The voice too has ceased.
Your translucent absence
fills this tent of glass.
This lifeless Venus,
her arm lost in history,
hides you from me.
This marble Sappho,
these Roman pillars,
Sumerian tablets, Assyrian icons,
the curves of hieroglyphs,
every wave from the past
stands between us,
a sea of forgetting.
I read your absence
in civilization's ruins;
I wander among angels
turning into devils
in the corridors of betrayal.
You are not among these gods
who died long ago,
nor these lutes and lyres
silenced in a bygone age.
Louvre is a huge graveyard of stillness
where Mona Lisa wryly smiles.
The Buddha too would have

smiled like this,
and you too, my intense one,
your hands raised
in the gesture of refuge,**
perhaps.

(*At Louvre Museum, Paris*)

16

I inhale your non-being
standing like the yaksha+
awaiting the cloud-messenger
on the top of this tower made of
steel, sweat, space and height.

The moist winds of young winter
Carry you, insubstantial, along with
the scent of lilies and hyacinths.
I stretch myself on your feathery absence
as on your breasts turgid with love.
Treading this emptiness I suddenly realise
you were the flesh of this skeletal tower
I scoop it up in my hands
like a throbbing heart.
My palm grows warm.
As I reach the square below
guarded by statues, your absence
melts into a winter shower
leaving its small footprints on the fallen leaves.

(At the Eiffel Tower)

17

After long years I again breathe
the prison's sighs to make sure
the world is still the same.

I know them: Liza, Farida, Bouvasse.
I see your face on everyone.
My poems will not brighten their nights;
Still I stammer about birth,
madness, prisons, revolutions...

Liza grips my hands tight·
'It's cruel, my brother, this prison.
I can't escape, so I too write,
for no one in particular.'

I too, sister. Writing is
a scream against walls.
It just bounces back;
yet we await the sun.
We are in the same half-dark solitude.
Solitude is the same everywhere,
the pale face of the winter-sun
behind the fog's curtain,
of the stonewall that doesn't permit
flowers and birthdays.

Solitude is a dumb hag,
wrinkled orphan.

Come, my sister,
I shall teach you to dance on embers
Like my father used to.
I too am on fire, dancing with
the skull in my hand, love-lorn.

(Poetry reading at the Central Jail, Paris)

18

Each country is a season.
Morning clings to my limbs.
I recall your curves like
autumn's yellow leaf recounting
the green veins of the spring leaf,
or a deer, shot, recalling
the thirsty spots of its mate
under another sky, in another forest.
I whistle towards you,
like a bird of passage in winter,
off on trembling wings
to a warm distant lake
through the icy tunnel of its songs.
Or like a dreaming snake,
or abear,
or me.

(*In Fontanableau forests*)

19

This river is Yamuna.⁺⁺
These willows bent towards yellow
Were kadamba trees in their previous birth.
A painter sketching the ancient bridge
is surprised by a pair of eyes
walking on the sea.
It is you, looking for
a shepherd, of words
I don't know magic,
yet I long to roll down from you,
a drop of tear that cannot play the flute.
I want to be cooled by these waters
until an artist scoops me up
to mix his paint and I am reborn
as colours on his canvas.
Then you will watch me with love
from this river in a ballet of eyelids.

(On the banks of river Loing, Moret)

20

Here they broke a prison open.
Was it freedom that leapt out, or solitude?
Now a theatre stands there.
Liberation is entertainment
when history is play.
Not even the pale recollections of 1968
in the sky of the Latin quarter.
Everything is quiet, desolate.
Do you remember, that summer
had warmed our adolescent Indian blood too.
How those purple songs grew dark
In the procession of the dead that followed!

Who am I talking to?
Are you my past, my present's absence?
Future is present's absence too.
I can imagine you as future's statue.
Perfect love is a spent coin,
Emptines brimming with milk,
Veiled height of love-bites, sky.

(At Bastille)

21

Time for mass in the church of Notre Dame.
These bells laugh like you.
And the choir wails like your absence.
Are you life, or death?
Don't know, nor do I wish to.
I know my cross, its weight.
I shall arrive there to
release me from myself,
to hand me over to love, entirely

(Notre Dame)

22

I am looking for the dear ones
in this cemetery of the labyrinths.
Here is Baudelaire, Here Maupassant,
Simone de Beauvoir, here Beckett,
Here Ionesco, here dear dear Cesar Vallejo...
Inspiration chokes the dead
trapped under stones.
I press my ears close to these decomposed dreams.
I can still hear their heart beats.
I know this tribe's dialect written
in every tongue since it has no alphabet.
Life without body can possess all flesh.
A gravestone with your name
suddenly rises to my eye.
'Where are you,' I scream.
Is this earth forgetting, is memory
the sky that buries birds?

Earth has no flowers
left for your tomb.

(At Montparnasse Cemeteries)

23

Picasso. Braque. Van Gogh. Degas.
Renoir. Dufy. Loutrec. Seurat.
Zola. Stendhal. Turgenev.
Truffaut. Tristan Tzara...
I chant these names in a chain
as if they still lived here, as if
my words have a rendezvous
with the rainbows and the dead.
The martyrs of the valley
with the lost memories of the Commune
rub shoulders with me:
moist winds with coffee smell.
On the steps of Sacre Cour, the wounded
Christ of Paris sobs like mist.
I look for you under each petal
of the pile of flowers on the street
that await the holy birth.
I look beneath every colour.
What is the colour of absence, white or black?
Tell me, the queen of jasmines,
tell me, rose's lyre, angel's bride,
tell.

(*At Montmartre*)

24

I don't want to see the arched triumph
of Napoleon, nor the dust the Nazis left.
I don't want to talk to the guillotines
O, Truffaut, Truffaut.
Who said, change is a wrath-driven beast?
Knowledge has a thousand apartments,
a thousand courtyards.

We cannot forget history, yet we have to
so that we open our eyes into light,
like new-borns cleaned of blood and muck,
so that we fly with the angels,
so that we love.

History is a place that does not exist.
And death, an epoch yet to excavate.

(At Champs Elysee)

25

Candles are plants with golden leaves.
They sprout and grow only
for those that bleed.
As they grow humility dwarfs them;
they shed their leaves and
drown in their own blood.
Candles are the prayers of the parted.
I too burn one as if you would
grow wings and suddenly land
among these saints and angels,
swooping down from the magic light
of thee stained-glass windows,
as if your non-being will slowly curdle
into being, in this cold, in this dark.

Love is prayer.
It burns in empty space.
This night I am drunk mad,
dancing in an abyss of live embers.
Several hands hold me.
I seek your face in everyone,
I kiss them as I would kiss you,
as our Black friend summons the strength
of all the forests into his drums.
Pain too climaxes with the drums.
I go on dancing with outstretched hands
and burning legs, hoping you would
emerge into light from this rhythm,

you would rise from flowers, from lamps,
from the screaming dust of abused streets,
from shadows, from laughters,
from wind or rain, from the scent of fruits,
from the other world of glass,
from crosses or graveyards,
from the incessant humming
of underground trains,
from the sudden blindnes of tunnels,
from piano's billows,
from the vigil of dances,
from the myriad hues of paintings,
from the drooping eyes of wine,
from poetry, from poetry, and
come into my hold from this
shivering 3 O'clock of the winter dawn.
I leap up in the joy of anticipation.

Wind round my neck,#
fall on my tangled hairs,
shine on my head,
O, word uttered by the mountains.
I sit in meditation for you, naked, ignorant
In the silence of the beginning,
in fire,
in fire.

(The farewell dance on the last day in Paris)

—

1997

* Paul Eluard's poem, 'Liberty.'
** Buddha's abhayamudra, a gesture offering refuge to the suffering.
+ In Kalidasa's *Meghadootam*, the hero, an ethereal yaksha in exile
awaits a cloud to carry his message to his beloved far away.
++ Yamuna is a river associated with Krishna, the flute-playing divine
lover. Kadamba trees are sacred to him.
There is an implied image of Lord Shiva here: he wears a serpent for
garland, has tangled hairs with the crescent moon in them where he
hides the river Ganga, his secret beloved. He dances on cremation
grounds with a skull in his hand. His consort Parvati is the daughter of
the Mount Himavant (Himalayas). She meditates and undergoes
penance in order to get Shiva for her husband. Note the reversal here.

IN ROOMS THAT CHOKE

When I die slowly
in rooms that choke
with you and breeze
and dreams and gods
all beyond my reach,
I call flowers by name.

When, one by one,
their scents fill my room,
I choke.

—

2001

IN YOU

When you were near me,
I thought love didn't need a body.
Now that you are away I know,
Love needs, like voice, a sky,
like water, a stream,
like electricity, a taut wire,
for me to be a cloud, a fish,
a warm tremor, in you.

Be my earth.
Let me blossom in your valleys,
their first blue flower.
Let me run whistling across your tunnels,
With a beacon on my brow.
Let me be a breeze in your woods,
a submarine in your seas.
I would be corn in your fields,
wander in your house
like the odour of mustard
bursting in oil.

I long to be born in you,
forever.

—

1994

INFINITE

I want to do with you
what spring does with cherry trees

— Pablo Neruda

1

The last drop of summer rain is
trickling on to the fallen mango leaf
pining beyond the window.
I am trying to unravel your mystery,
gathering your letters, nail marks
and the odours of your body
like a Sherlock Holmes decoding
fingerprints, rose petals,
manuscripts and poison vials.
I recreate your contours
like a drunk driver sighting a rainbow
across the distancing glass.
In the end, with irrepressible fervour,
I hug everything I come by:
The moist robes of rutting autumn,
the half-blossomed bunch of *rajanigandha*,
Kafka's letters to Milena,
Lorca's ballads,
Ramanan,[1]
Mona Lisa.

2

It was a summer evening.
You quietly placed your palm on mine
like God polishing a rainbow
and placing it in the azure sky.

What did the promise mean?
—that we will walk, rain-drenched,
splashing water from the puddles
along the side-lanes of a childhood spring
that we failed to share?
—that we will, through an electrifying kiss,
transmit to each other the whole
uneasy history of our past travails?
—that your ears will emit the scent of jasmines
As my lips turn into an intense breeze
and murmur, 'love is an eternal quarrel with an angel?'[2]
—that, through the night, flinging
our robes of shame into fire,
we will taste the wild honey of
nocturnal flowers with our eager tongues?

3

You are that lean eleven-year old,
fleeing the bomb in Vietnam.
As the dry-leaved lanes of your village caught fire,
You ran naked, leaving your blazing body
to the wind and the sun.
It was to my breast which had lulled
hunger to sleep you came.
Among the scars of many battles,
I had set aside for you
a barrel of words to quench the fire,
a drop of honey for your burnt heart
and a sun flower seed for tomorrow.

Don't say we are on two planets,
that our dancing feet are shackled.
Don't say it is from within the rocks
that we dream of leaves and birds.

You were mine since you were born.
I grew these thorns waiting for you.
Yet only the springs deep beneath the sands
can fill the dates with sweetness.

4

Lulled by the rose-like caress of a cool breeze,
we walked by the dreaming lake
that lay like a peacock feather.
Your heart throbbed in my hands
in the blushing memories
of a night of honey and acid.

My lips had four rainbows;
and your breasts, four clouds.
The starnds of your hair
scribbled on my pillow: 'Your scent, dear,
I will carry to my garden.'
My tongue whispered to your tiny belly:
'I long to sprout inside you,
I want to be born in a war-free world.'

You sobbed over the children
massacred in Baslan; I fell in fragments
into the last vineyards from the
blown roof of Baghdad.
A cigarette-butt, flung by God,
winked at me: 'You have
three more nights to celebrate your survival.'

5

You place a red *manchadi* seed on my brow.
I roll a pearl along your navel.
I rub your nipples with
the honey of banana blooms.
You place a purple *manganari* flower
On my lips and blow
a couplet of Tukaram onto my breast,
I worship your eyes with a leaf from
The poetry of Ezhuthacchan.
I say: Matisse
You say: Beethoven
I say: Van Gogh
You say: Mozart
I say: Picasso
You say: Stravinsky
I say: Brecht
You say: Kumar Gandharv
I say: Vallejo
You say: Ramanathan
I say: Love.
You say: Love.

I raise you to the moon like a goblet.
Then we kiss, toasing the whole creation.
You come back, a rainbow

round your neck, a star in your hair.

You say: Sky
I say: Sea
Blue envelopes us.
Blue music. Blue moonlight.
Blue you. Blue me.
Blue ecstasy.

6

I am reading to you the lines of Ritsos:
'I know it is very late now. Let me come
because for so many years I've remained alone'[3]

I thought you would speak of
Rilke's lion or Mallarme's swan;
but you were thinking of love,
that fairest of gods.

7

Why were you born so late?
In which star were you, in which water?
In which sunrise, in which fear of mankind?

No, love never comes late;
it annihilates years and ages,
falls like lightning at the centre of Time.
Then sitting on tombstones
It murmurs the nostalgic lines of Celan:
'Your golden hair, Margarete,
your ashen hair, Shulamith...'⁴

O, your straight hair drives me mad.
like the greedy soldiers back home
from the warfront, driving their vans
again and again along the counryside,
my fingers grope lustily
along those black lanes
for a broken bangle-shard,
a drop of moonlight,
a forgotten lullaby.

Your bubbling lips drive me mad.
I return to them over and over
like a drunkard to his wine.

I come back to your firm breasts
Like a devotee to the marmoreal idol
of his household goddess.
I come back to your burning navel
like the offering to the sacrificial fire.
I am the offering, the first man.
You are the fire, the first woman and the last,
limitless and timeless.
You are Gauri, Aruna, Bhargavi, Medini.
I am the hibiscus blossoming in the tribal hamlet
chanting your thousand names,
aching to attain your lap.

8

I have been travelling to you
through many half-lit births.
You have many names: Radha, Urvashi,
Laila, Anarkali, Leela, Chandrika:
each one a sunflower I half-bloom.
I do not want Juliet nor Cleopatra;
I want the thorny one, one likeme,
flowering in the desert,
remembering everything, sharing everything:
pain, madness, words, thoughts,
body, soul, everything.

Daughter of legends, carry me
away from this world
growing dreadful day by day
for those who are not yet blind
into the moonlight of *ranjini,*[5]
the valley of pianos.

Look, Bob Dylan has turned into moonlight;
each tree swaying in the breeze, his guitar.

9

Where did you bury that red mark
my teeth had left on your right breast?
Did you lend it to the evening sky?
All the birds criss-crossing the sky grow red.
Leaves, flowers, streams, hills, all red.
A red moon bends over a red sea.
Tomorrow's sun wll be red too.

How a bedsheet turns into
Vatsyayana in a single night![6]
Love too is meditation,
in twenty-four postures.

10

'Like the red earth and the pouring rain...'
a simile steps out from
the pages of the *Kurunthokai*.[7]
We are so mixed and kneaded
no drought can separate us.
I am there in your each drop,
and you in my each grain.

You are a bamboo bush.
As I blow through you,
each of your pores exudes Chaurasia's music.

You are a palette. My mad fingers
spread your colours on the canvas
like a Paul Klee painting.
Your anklet resounds in all my words;
The flapping of your wings
echoes in all my seasons.
This moist book you have kept open for me,
Is it *Geetgovind* or *Gathasaptasati*?[8]

11

There are many birds in your throat.
One, a parrot, another a mynah.
When you sleep, they return to the woods.
When I see you sleeping in the nude,
I recall Hiroshima. I remove
the glass shards from your flesh
and wipe away the clotted blood.

You are every woman, the one
abandoned in the forest, the one
buried in backwaters, stoned on the street,
burnt at the stake, poisoned, exchanged,
beloved, bride, widow, whore.

Let me kiss your contended body
for all the flowers that failed
to blossom on earth, for lovers and refugees.

O, my Magdalene,
I who am no Jesus.

12

Now half-asleep, we are listening to Kabir.[9]
Rama relinquishing the throne
puts his arms on our shoulders
and sings of the body free of insignia
and of unqualified love.
He invites us to the Infinite.
I peer into the nightsky of your eyes.
where a crescent moon plays violin.
Come, let me lie in your lap this moment.

I wish to hear the sea billow like
Kumar Gandharv singing Tukaram's *abhang*.[10]

13

You are reading poetry from the dais,
with the same lips I had drunk from last night.
My hands become a breeze caressing your hair.
Each emerging word carries a kiss's wet seal.
We don't see the audience.
Let the world vanish; your words are only for me.
How everyone's language becomes
ours alone in certain moments!
Every noun becomes an olive branch extended to me,
every adjective, a wing, every verb ticks
like a clock measuring the span of love.

Ask the synonyms to leave us alone,
let us talk staright.

In the madness of odours, I jump into you.
You are the wildest of rivers,
the ever-billowing sea, the journey of the salt
beyond Babel, the vigil of the spark
beneath the ash.

14

Tell the sun not to rise tomorrow.
Tell the door not to open into the world's hurry.
Tell the bed not to betray us to the daylight.
Your cheeks are red like an arch on flame.
I see you as a tiny girl in a little white skirt,
in plaited hair, with a tender coconut-leaf
in your hand, on your way to the church
holding your mother's hand.
I see you taller in full skirt, waiting for the bus
in the village square. Had you noticed me then,
fluttering about you as a butterfly?
A sparrow I had watched you
from the window-sill of your college class room.
Every step you took was towards me.

I am scared. Night will come tomorrow too.
O, the night of blood and devils,
in hell, without you.

Before we part, pour into my words:
that mixed fragrance unique to you, of
white lilies and hot chillies;
that rare voice of swallows twittering
over the rushing rainwater below;
that touch of your long fingers that passes

to each follicle the message of a cyclone;
that taste of your secrets, of *champa* blossoms
or of the pink flesh of pomegranate,
I will never know.

Then I can look straight at the solar eclipse
of this terrible century: until there remains
in my blinded eyes only, only,
your beloved image.

—

2005

---

[1] A popular pastoral elegy in Malayalam by Changampuzha Krishna Pillai

[2] Jaroslav Seifert: 'Struggle with an Angel.'

[3] Yannis Ritsos: 'Moonlight Sonata.'

[4] Paul Celan: 'Death Fugue.'

[5] ranjini: a raga in Carnatic music.

[6] Remember Vatsyayana's Kamsootra, dealing with postures in love.

[7] Kurunthokai: an anthology of Tamil classical poetry

[8] Geetagovindam, a 14th cent. Erotic-devotional poem in Sanskrit by Jayadeva, Gathasaptasati, an anthology of erotic lovepoetry in Prakrit collected by King Hala.

[9] Kabir, the 16th cent. devotional poet, a weaver by profession, a critic of status quoist religion.

[10] Abhang is a verse form popularised by Tukaram, the 17th cent. Marathi saint-poet

INTENSE

Forget the key and remain a child
Adorn the ears with a red hibiscus
Bathe in the wild stream and eat the berry
Drop anchor in the moon and go to sleep
  Remember your mother

Pray sitting on the leopard's back
Learn to walk on the burning pyre
Kiss the king cobra's hood
Play the sun and sing the Blues
Roll the sea and smoke
  Remember your father

Turn the heart into a wasp's nest
Play chess with the dark
Flirt with the flood
Set fire to your waist
Make a knife of gold
  Remember your love

Climb the hill of insomnia,
Write on the wall with burning coal
Beat your skin to awaken the lion
Pierce words with a trident
Ride Tomorrow's back
  Remember your friend

Turn the banyan into a palace
Write a hymn in blood from the cross
Aim an arrow at memory's feet
Peel off your body and flee
Pay your debts by drinking venom
   Remember your foe

Stand guard to the door of the earth
Hold the reins of the sky
Wear the river around your neck
Tattoo the forest on your chest
Lend your heart throbs to emptiness
   Remember your God

God is not outside Time,
Just as not the pine, the fish, the cloud.
Nothing He created accompanies Him
When His time ends
He will fall from the East,
A window on fire,
In Auschwitz where poison
Fumes and screams
Or in Gaza's dust
Red with children's blood,
Like those corpses of the innocent
That daily fall on our plates of food
With the burnt fingers of babies.

—

2015

INVISIBLE

I have never seen you;
may be I never will.
Still I know you are there,
like some unseen stars,
like the first wonder-filled flap
of the just-created bird,
like some half-formed words
on the frontiers of language,
like some planets,
fuming fluid yet.

2

Your crystal-voice
quickens my heartbeat,
like coffee, like pepper,
like jazz, like drugs.

3

You are a dripping tunnel
with light at the end.
I long to get wet
passing through you
listening to the songs
of the forest-birds
that thrill the wind.

4

The scent of how many flowers
from your body shining far-away
is igniting my senses?

5

Let those hands keep moving,
their bangles laughing,
shaping the fragile idols of love.

6

Who said life is a tree
that blossoms just once
and then dries up?
This is that moment,
unrepeatable, of blossoming.

7

I am a grain of sand
and you, the endless sea.
Let me multiply and be the earth
to contain all of you?

8

I tremble all over like
the tallest building
in a quake-hit city.
You are the oldest of its roads.
Split open so that I may
tumble down to be
devoured by your womb
and open my fresh eyes
into the light of a city
yet to be born.

—
2012

LOVE-BUDDHA

'Which is the sweetest kiss on earth?,'
once you threw me a puzzle.
'Is it the feather-like kiss that the mother
gives the baby she had just lulled
to sleep, careful not to wake it up?
Is it the first burning kiss the lover gives
his beloved as they stand on either side
of a sunflower melting its gold?
Or the last kiss the widow places
on the dead lips of her husband,
moist with the tears of parting?
Is it the sacred dispassionate kiss
the young hermit piously places
on the newly-washed feet of his Guru?
Or the ceaseless green kisses that the wind
gives the tree, the leaf gives the little bird,
the sun gives the forest, the moonlight gives
the river and the rain gives the mountains?'

I can answer it now.
Mist has a house above Devikulam.
On one side is the rushing emerald of the valley
and on the other, the primal grandeur
of rocks as ancient as the earth.
Hidden by the rocks is a cave
filled with darkness and mystery.

Inside it I kissed you, witnessed by the mixed
fragrance of thirty-seven nameless wild flowers.
It had the first kiss and the last one;
You were baby, beloved and widow.
I became wind, leaf, sun, moon and rain.
Time shrunk into a brief moment.
Our kiss flashed like a lightning in the dark.
That cave became Bodhi; I was illumined
by love's revelation.

Now I travel through births.
I will attain the Supreme State only after
the last human pair has found love's salvation.

—

1985

LOVING A WOMAN

To love a woman is
to resurrect her from stone,
to fondle her from tip to toe
until her blood frozen by curse
is warmed by a dream.[1]

To love a woman is
to turn her soot-laden day
into a skylark that breathes
the flower-dust of paradise;
to turn oneself into a tree in bloom
for her tired wings to rest at night.

To love a woman is
to set sail on a storm-swept sea
under an overcast sky
in search of a new continent;
to carry a red balsam
from your frontyard to an unseen shore
and plant it there.

To love a woman is
to exchange the harshness of your muscles
for the tenderness of a flower,[2]
to free yourself of the armour and the crown,
bare, cross another sky

and leave your flesh to the winds
of another planet, to another water.

To love a woman is
to help her unearth a ray-sharp sword
from her ancient scars
and lie pressing your heart on its blade
until you are drained of all your blood.

I have never loved a woman.

—

1992

[1] Remember the tale of Ahalya turned into a stone by the curse of her
husband the Rishi Viswamitra and restored by Rama.
[2] Bhima, the strongest of the Pandavas, was sent to the forest by
Draupadi, the wife of the five brothers, to fetch the Saugandhika flower
that he did, overcoming many obstacles.

MON AMOUR*

I hug you with my eyes
you caress me with your wounds
I peel off your garments
you wipe off your bloodstains
I suck your lips
your acid burns mine
I taste your tongue
your untold tales sour my mouth
I rouse your nipples
you mourn your estranged son
I run my fingers across your belly
you start as if recalling a rape
I play on your behind
it grows heavy with distances
I press my lips on your petals
you remind me of our orphaned kids
I enter you
you scream like an embattled city
I raise you to the rainbows
you climax in a rain of bombs
I break and scatter in you
my sharpnels pierce you

Love bleeds in prisons.

—
2001

*'My love.' Remembering Alan Resnais's film, *Hiroshima mon amour*

NAINI

(Nainital, 10 June 2004)

This lake is goddess Parvati's eye
open to Mount Kailas,[1]
its blue dense with the love
of a lifetime's penance.
Fishes and canoes pass
across these liquid dreams.
Trees see their future
mirrored in this blue.

The breeze whispers
a Pahari folksong[2]
about love in my ears.
My love for you grows
amidst these mountains.
This chill burns.

Back in the room,
I find I have a third eye:
the instinct's eye to feel
the orgasm of animals.[3]
I grow a trunk in the
lustful memory of the forests.

We now need a black calf
that can smell the vanished flowers
and wave its ears to the
lost drum-beats' rhythms.

I regret having burnt alive
Kama, the lord of love.[4]

—

2004

[1] Parvati, the daughter of Himavan (Mount Himalayas personified), won the love of Lord Shiva through a long meditative penance. Nainital is in the Himalayas; Mount Kailas, sacred to Shiva too.

[2] Pahari is a Himalayan language as well as a Hindustani raga.

[3] It is said that Shiva and Parvati turned into various animals in love-play to know their orgasm and Lord Ganapati with his elephant's head and man's body was born after the couple had made love in the form of elephants.

[4] Shiva had once burnt the love-god Kama (the Cupid of Indian mythology) to ashes by opening his third eye for arousing his desire for Parvati by shooting his flower-arrows and later revived him when he married Parvati.

NAME

What is the name of that star,
you asked me.
Knowledge won't do for love, I said.
You knew me, instantly.

What is the name of that star,
you asked me.
You smell of cinnamon,
I said.

What is the name of that star,
you asked me.
Venus and Hesperus
are your names, I said.

The warriors set out
to welcome Future
were coming back, blinded.
You threw away everything:
your clothes, your pain,
your solitude.
I raised you to my lips:
A toast for the Future that will never be.
You turned into a star.

What is my name,
you asked.

The Last Star,
I said.

—

1994

ON THE WAY TO SHILLONG

On the way to Shillong
on the sepia banks of Umiyam lake
under a jacaranda tree in bloom
I saw her: Banalata Sen.*

Today after a decade
I again pass by the lake.
She is still there:
A jacaranda tree in full bloom
under a violet cloud
scurrying along the sky.

—
2003

*The protagonist of Jibanananda Das's Bengali poem, *Banalata Sen*

RAIN IN KOCHI

Walking in the rain
with you, I held my palm
above your head.
You pushed it aside,
got soaked in the rain
and grew shoots.
Then you put on leaves,
boughs, flowers and fruits.
I long to roost on your boughs
and spread my wings.
But this rain drenching even my dreams
will soak my feathers
and go on still,
bloating me out,
and you too.

—

1998

RAIN, YOU

Was it rain
or you?

There were scents:
intense ones,
of the rain-washed earth, of tobacco,
of the acrid sap of the mango-stalk,
of oleander flowers,
of woman's inner lips.

There were colours,
flying ones,
of the mynah, of the pink balsam,
of collyrium, of wild fire,
of wet yam leaves, of red wine,
of fresh paddy.

There were memories,
unendurable ones,
of the index finger, wet lips,
aroused nipples,
wounds, bells,
irreplaceable hearts.

How many names how many selves
How many places how many births
How many rivers from touches

The mad ecstasy of dreaming of your return
when I lose you
The wild shock of the fear of losing you
when you return.

I have never seen a rain so blue
an embrace so liquid, a dance so irrepressible,
a monsoon kiss that rains so incessantly
like flowers from a *gulmohar* tree.

—

2005

REPETITIONS

We make love on the beach
and re-enact the ritual
in signs scrawled on the sand:
'We made love here.'

The wind, waves and indifferent feet
conspire in envy to tear that
festival banner apart.

Love's evanescence
deposits salt in the follicles of
our hair, all on end.

Tomorrow another pair
will land up here: man
and woman; may be man
and man, or woman
and woman: they too
will scrawl that line
on the shifting sand;
the same salt-breeze
will sing for them a lullaby.

Love is not eternal;
it just ceaselessly repeats itself,
saltily, like the sea.

—
2011

REUNION

A man can recognize his first love
even when meeting her
after a gap of thirty years:
like recognizing his ancestral house
in the village despite the renovations;
like recognizing the desolation
of his old hill wrapped in wild flowers
even after it has been covered with
buildings and the tumult of crowds.

He tries to recreate their first meeting
like remembering his place in the
school photo eaten up by silverfish.

A festival rages in his mind;
but the drum-beats fail to cross
the high temple walls.
He wants to hold her beloved head
close to his chest and let her listen
to all the passing clatter
of his last thirty years
and to touch and smell
her heavens and hells.

But there is an ocean
between them now.
Watching the marks of time's
sculpting on her body
he asks her in a tone of forced
detachment: 'How are you?'
Noting the slashes and scars of
years on him she responds: 'Fine.'

They choke like two corpses
trying to talk to each other
from their coffins.
They move away from each other
unable to bear the impossible weight
of earth and rocks and trees above.

Between them remains
only, only, the ocean.

—

1998

SHAKUNTALAM

Every lover is cursed
to forget, at least for a while,
his woman: as the river of
amnesia devours his love.

Every beloved is cursed
to be forgotten until her secret
is trapped in the net of memory.

Every child is cursed
to grow fatherless,
with his hand in the lion's mouth.

—

2003

SOME KINDS OF LOVE

Some kinds of love are like flu.
First you sneeze, your body aches all over
you are hot outside and inside.
It subsides after a week of nightmares;
now you are in forgetful repose.

Some kinds of love are like smallpox.
You wonder whether
what you see on your skin
are blisters or gooseflesh.
Your body is red-hot with love
You may survive it, but
the pockmarks remain.
You carry those scarred memories
on your body until you die.

Some kinds of love are like cancer.
You take time to diagnose it.
The pain starts too late.
By the time she is already
someone else's.
The drugs to stop that love-cell
from multiplying in vain
will turn you thin and pale
like the proverbial lover.

When indifference fails,
a knife alone can save you.
Maimed thus, you live like dead.
When it spreads again
death kindly tempts you from
the branch of a tree, a river,
a tall balcony or a small bottle.
Love survives you.

Some kinds of love are like madness.
You are lost entirely
in a world of imagination;
your beloved does not even
know of your love.
You murmur, sing, laugh, quarrel
and roam around, all, alone.
Neither shackles nor electric shocks
can tame it, for, it is no disease,
but is a state of dream;
hence it lives among the stars.

The sweetest love is
the unrealised one,
like Radha's.

—

2016

SULEKHA

With so many wings, Sulekha,
what are you doing there?
The white robe of a divine bride,
white rose, white dreams: I see everything.

You are the foster-child of
sacrificial altars, the ancient
fragrance of intense springs,
the desperate, transparent, smile of glass.

Every night you come, borne on
the bitter winds of salt fields;
you show me your wounds
like mist, and sob.

The winter night trembling by the window
is pale like garlic.
The leaves of cancer that unfold in
your funeral pyre look brown.
The scent of *palai* and *arali* flowers dissolves
in the pungent smell of burning corpses.

You too should have sought shelter here,
In this moonlight, under this
mushroom of mist.
But that fat sticky beast that

inhabits the darkest of wells
stood between us. Was it
the same beast that entered
your innards and multiplied?

What was it the flames of the pyre
whispered in your tiny ears,
as they stroked your dead hairs
with fingers of gold?
What was the song the fire sang,
with you in his lap,
caressing and fondling you until
your bones exploded in a fit of passion?

Sulekha, you came into the world too early.
Even sunflowers have claws and fangs here.
Prisons open to receive patriots,
like the black books of judgement.
Sterile winds roll over
the broken bones of the just.

Be reborn one day on the fragrant earth
as the first shower raising
the stimulating scent of the rain-drenched soil.
Flow laughing like the water from the eves
beneath the neem tree on the courtyard.

Then a child will clap his hands and laugh
launching a paper-boat on your breast.
A red-breast will fly above you
on his flushed wings, like an arrow.

That bird will be me.

–

1981

THE ASCENT

Climb no more I can; my legs ache
and a night thickens in my eyes.
A ghost-like fog slithers out of the cave,
its stare stony and its claws sharp.
It freezes the sun within my head,
freezes the garden within my heart.
Numb go the stars of my spine and
numb the goldfish of my veins.
My nerves' horses fell dead on the way.
Is it death I smell in the air, my love?

1

Once like grasshoppers we leapt up
on the green valley's breast;
the dewdrops on our wings turned
into the emeralds of heaven.
Once we bathed in the rain with not
a mushroom above our heads;
we danced in the sun with not
a tender leaf around our waists.
You were fruit and I was its sweetness;
you were the silver stream and I was
its rainbow-fish. You were glass and
I was light; you breeze and I the dry leaf,
you deer and I your spot. How tender
the days had been like moonlight's plumes
as we enacted the tale of evolution!

2

Then came the bear. It growled.
'Rain,' we thought, and crept under
the blankets. It knocked on our door.
'Wind,' we said, and closed the windows tight.
It came and in our backyard stood,
'Night,' we went back to sleep.
And at midnight as we wake up,
Isn't it the bear beneath our bed?
Its bristles prick our groping hands. When
did he climb up, to lie between you and me?

At dawn I look into the mirror and start
to see my body covered in fur.
I put on a full-sleeve to hide the fur
and growl: 'Bring me tea, quick!'
Did you, my love, see my blood-stained fangs
when I opened my mouth to sip the tea?
Or had you seen it on our bridal night
as I parted my lips to kiss you welcome?
Did they grow longer and sharper
In the daily relish of your tender flesh?
Mouth closed I stroll along the street,
growling, gloating over the wild honey you gave.
No man I come across is without a fang:
Perplexed I turn to a friend who quips:
'What's a male without a fang?
Isn't it manhood's flag, like the fur,
the claws and the growl?'

3

Did you sob at night and rave in sleep:
'Won't that time come back ever?
Call me please, just once more, in that voice
as soft as the first shoots of spring.
Kiss me once like you did then, with those
moonlight's lips, unstained by blood.
Praise me not in poetry; just hold me
as I fall all sweat in the kitchen-soot.
Just come close and caress my imprisoned flesh
Weep once like rain, burst out laughing
like a bunch of the white *palai* blooms.
Let's be filled with the festive hues
and flavours the childhood held.'

I shook you awake, and you said:
'A mountain I saw in my dream.
Come, let's go there. Your friends can never
scale those heights nor nightmares haunt
you there; you won't hear the screams
of sacrificial infants there nor see
the strange mercies that offer you
a cup of poison as you thirst.
It's always full moon there, leaves that
never fall and flowers that never fade.
Its streams are molten gold and

its huge rocks, diamonds.
The lamb tickles the lion-cub there and
the serpent befriends the mongoose.
There is, in that land, a blue, blue lake
beneath a ruby mount that melts
in the forefathers' living breath.
Dip in that lake, rise with a pebble
in your hands and whatever wish you make
with that stone becomes real.
Come, let's wish an earth ever free
from poverty, disease and death!'

4

Climb no more I can;
the air here is rare and the wind
freezes even the marrow.
Death is afoot, it comes from my skull,
from my life-dissolving breath.
I won't reach those heights, my love,
I already inhale the pyre's smoke.
Let me bid you farewell here,
my head on your lap, in the shade
of this birdsong, in the greenest of
meadows that oozes breastmilk!
Plant a banyan seedling here and
climb the rest alone. Throw my ashes too
into that blue crystal lake up there.

Close your eyes and wish an earth where
man is no more woman's hell.
Wish pure air and water and unbounded
spirit for those yet unborn.

Then you will see a flock of birds above
and you will see me, one among them.
A cluster of stars will brighten the clouds
and I will see you, one among them.

—
1990

THE DANCE

1

I remember you like
the misplaced key
remembering its locked house.

You come to me rushing,
a gurgling spring from the buried rivers
with a city's clamour.

A dream in gold and brown
stealthily enters history
from the canvas where
goddesses keep on blooming.

Birds flap their wings
under the frozen sea.

The sky is green,
corpses fast like arrows.

2

You are all the colours.

You are red and black:
a rose of blood,
night's lone wing.

You are blue and green:
the ocean's endless lotus,
the grasshopper God rides on earth.

You are yellow and brown:
The daylight's dance on the sunflowers,
The sky of the mynahs.

You are saffron and gold:
The sea of kumkum flowers,
The full moon on the beach.

No white, please.

3

This is a house of mirrors.
Each mirror reflects
one of your selves.

You are besieged by yourself,
you drew your form out of you
It shrank, swelled, multiplied.
Who am I among these countless images,
am I their brush, or the palette?

I am disembodied here,
a mere orphan soul,
a buried village,
a blocked street.

4

Prise me open,
draw out from the ice of oblivion
trapped streets, ricefields,
megaliths, mothergoddesses,
possessed dancers,
all the streams entangled in thorns,
all the festivals dried up in the sand,
all the legends frozen before they were told,
all the ringing bells
echoed by bird's nests,
all the hands planted in the soil,
all the grammar of the forests.

There is a lioness in your eyes.
And in the eyes of that lioness,
me.

5

The one born to language in colour,
my words are your canvas,
your silence is my paper.

Fill the empty goblets once again
make your lines dance
fill your colours with God
invoke the One
who is neither man nor woman,
who has neither race nor religion,
whose body is the universe,
who is realised in the abstract.

Fill, get filled,
dance in colours,
on earth,
in the sky,
in water,
in fire,
in the mind,
in time,
in the timeless.

—
2009

THE HAND

You placed your hand in my hand:
as the sky does on earth.
Children exclaimed
the curry-leaf plant had flowered.
Four cranes rose from the bamboo bush
and flew across the clouds.
A rainbow gleamed above the hedgerow.
The river licked our feet and
lay curled under the table.
We reached Mount Kailash
hanging on to a sentence
that had descended from the sky.

Your body was all wet;
my wings had grown red.
Now the words of that sentence
grew into trees and
hid us from the eyes of God.

—

2004

THE HOME AND THE PRISON

You brought a sunflower's seed,
and I, a daylight's leaf.
You brought a fistful of moonlight
and I, a night of dance.
You brought a doe's tears,
and I, a wild wasp's honey.
You brought a feather of Paradise,
and I a word of God.
Our house was white,
and our babies dark.
They cried; I couldn't bear,
I flew to the sun for a grain of rice.

Now my wings and my songs
are locked up in this cloud.
My solitude speaks in the thunder,
and with the lightning
I grope for our home.

When it grows cold, my song
melts into a shower, falling
over our white house,
over the dark void between us.

—

1985

TO PROLONG THE NOON

To prolong the noon I sit
sipping beer on this final beach.

The wind and I get a high as we
see in your eyes the glitter
of our first days together.
The sea, endless like death,
Takes no notice.

The refrain of birds above
like a new song earth has learnt.

My childhood is a top that got
buried in the sand even before
it had begun to spin.

Once I heard a tempest's echoes
in a sparrow's twitter.
No, we cannot check
this growing chill.

Joy is a goblet
flung into the dark.
And love, a kite
put out among the clouds.

—

2000

WHEN I ENTER YOU

When I enter you,
I am entering a gorge
God had opened for me
in Syria's Maloola.
To arrive there I travelled along
clay-hills and wet valleys,
along words, thirsts and songs.

I know this moist red earth
and this pouring rain.

Someone is pursuing me
with an open sword,
that is why I speed up
even on this slippery terrain.

Palm trees and camels
should not see me.
I should reach the land beyond
before night arrives.

Here, I am rising,
to the rainbow with
eighteen colours.

Lord,
your country has come.

—

2014

WHISPERS

What I spoke was all about blood
and you, about roses.
Which alchemy of memory
gave your roses the colour of my blood
and my blood the fragrance of your roses?

2

Your letter was a seashore.
In some of its lines love glistened
like iron ore in the sand.
I caught them with my eyes' magnet and
left the rest for the waves.

3

I gifted a kerchief carrying my name
to the breeze that absorbed your sweat.
It came back with a butterfly
you had embroidered—
to where butterflies had vanished
even from dreams.

4

There is a wolf on your shoulders,
a cobra in your hair
a vulture in your eyes.
I fear your desire, darling,
your youth that shines like a dagger,
the sun in the pit of your navel,
your unquenchable hunger
opening its red mouth like a fledgling bird.
Is your vehicle horse or lion?

5

What was the language
in which you were raving
when you climaxed?
Each hot breath a word,
each brief scream a sentence.
The climax of pain has no dictionary
and the climax of pleasure, no grammar.

6

I used to be proud that
I knew your body's map by heart.
Who redrew its borders? Who
partitioned it? Where are the water-falls,
the hills, the lanes?
I roam the wrong passages,
step into the wrong house,
I lose my way.

7

Your name has become a stone in my kidneys.
More solid than pain.
More brown than memory.
I carry it as I walk, bent,
pressing my belly down.
Great surgeons of the world,
don't bother to unlodge it,
let her dear name stuck in my body
deliver me from sins.

8

You are a myth; so you don't like similes.
The spring of metaphors has dried up;
now it oozes only blood.
In that too is your warm red name.
It sings, blood sings,
blood is Rumi.

—
2017

YOUR LIPS

Your lips are red hot.
I kiss them, my lips turn into
a noon, scorching.

Your lips are an oozing honeycomb.
I stroke them; a thousand wasps
besiege my heart.

Your lips are the crimson dawn
of my lost dreams. They touch my eyes;
their summer sun dazzles my vision.

Your lips are acidic quills.
They carve your name
on my brow, forever.

Your lips are the windstorms of June.
They pass over my body, rousing
dust, water, poetry, all at once.

Your lips are this coast and that.
I launch my tremulous tongue
on the torrent between them.

Your lips are a pair of tiny red wings.
My lips soar on them
to the timeless blue.

Your lips are the shores of the red sea.
I sit on them to meditate,
watching the daylight in repose.

Your lips are birth and death.
My being gets choked
between them.

I pass from this world
to the other along these scarlet bridges.

Your lips are silk, rose, rainbow, breeze,
water, plum, feather, ecstasy.

From between your lips emerge
love, fire, spring, moonlight,
children, breast milk.

Your lips are *sa* and *sa*.
between them lie the seven notes of music,
crescendo and decrescendo, all the *ragas*,
named and unnamed.

Your lips are alpha and omega.
Between them lie the alphabet, all words.
I pick some of them with my lips,
and put them together.
I call it poetry, you call it love.
In truth it is a soul, a lean spirit
that comes out of hellfire, burnt:
Dante, Paul Celan, Edappilly.*

—

2004

*Edappilly Raghavan Pillai: a Malayalam romantic poet driven to
suicide by poverty and failure in love.

K. SATCHIDANANDAN

K.Satchidanandan (born on 28 May 1946) is an Indian poet, essayist, playwright, travel-writer and translator writing in Malayalam, the language of Kerala and a bilingual (Malayalam and English) critic and editor. He has been Professor of English at Christ College, University of Calicut, Kerala, editor of *Indian Literature*, the journal of the Sahitya Akademi (The National Academy of Letters) and later the Chief Executive of the Akademi. He then worked as a Language Policy Consultant for the Government of India and has been associated as editor with *Katha*, Delhi and the Foundation of SAARC Writers and Literature. He edits the poetry quarterly *Kerala Kavita* in Malayalam and has edited a series of selections of poems by distinguished Malayalam poets and a series of translations from South Asian literature, *The South Asian Library of Literature* in English besides several collections of poetry and essays including *Words Matter*, an anthology of dissent published by Penguin India. He retired in 2011 as Director and Professor, School of Translation Studies and Training, Indira Gandhi National Open University, Delhi. He was also on the Project Advisory Board of *Indian Literature Abroad*, and the National Executive of the *National Translation Mission* and has been on the Executive Board of Sahitya Akademi besides being on the academic/governing bodies of JNU, (Delhi), Ambedkar University (Delhi), Malayalam University (Kerala) and has been on the PhD board of four universities. Until recently he was a National Fellow at the Indian Institute of Advanced Study, Shimla and is a Distinguished Member, Loka Kerala Sabha, Member, Kerala State Higher Education Board and Co-Chairman for Art and Literature, Kerala State Planning Board. He is also the Director of the Kerala Literature Festival.

Satchidanandan has 27 collections of poetry in Malayalam, 16 collections of world poetry in translation, four plays, three books of travel and 23 collections of critical essays and interviews besides five collections of essays in English. He has edited several anthologies of poetry and prose in Malayalam, English and Hindi. He has 33 collections of his poems in translation in 18 languages, including seven collections in English, the chief of them being *While I Write* (HarperCollins), *Misplaced Objects and Other Poems* (Sahitya Akademi), *The Missing Rib* and *Not Only the Oceans* (Poetrywala), eight in Hindi, four in Tamil, two in Kannada, two in Oriya, two in Assamese, two in Marathi and one each in Irish, Arabic, Chinese, Japanese, German, French, Italian, Bengali, Telugu and Gujarati. He has won 52 awards and honours for his literary contribution including Bharatiya Bhasha Parishad Award, Gangadhar Meher Award and Kavisamrat Upendra Bhanja Award, Kerala Sahitya Akademi Award (5 times, for different genres), Kumaran Asan Award, Bapureddy National Award, N T Rama Rao National Award, Kuvempu National Award, Kusumagraj National Award, Kerala Varma

Award, Ulloor Award, P. Kunhiraman Nair Award (twice), Odakkuzhal Award, Vayalar Award, SBT Suvarna Mudra, Padmaprabha Puraskaram, V. Aravindakshan Award, Kavyotsav Award, Hariyorma Award, Kesari Nayanar Award, first Kamala Surayya Memorial award, Navamalayali Award, Kerala SSF award and Ezhuthachan Award, the topmost award for any writer in Kerala, Kadammanitta Ramakrishnan Award, Baharain Keraleeya Samajam Award, Oman Kerala Cultural Centre Award, Kamala Surayya Award, UA Exchange Award, Sahitya Akademi Award for Malayalam, Kala award for total contribution from London, and Poetry for Peace Award from the Govt. of UAE. He has also won Green India Excellence Award for environmental writing besides Sahityasree from the Hindi Sahitya Sammelan, Delhi, Senior Fellowship from the Department of Culture, Government of India, Sreekant Verma Fellowship from the Government of Madhya Pradesh and the K.K.Birla Fellowship for Comparative Literature. He is a Fellow of the Kerala Sahitya Akademi. Many of his books of poetry and criticism have been textbooks in Universities and there are several PhDs on his poetry. A film on him, *Summer Rain* was released in 2007. His name was in the Ladbroke list of the first ten probable winners of the Nobel Prize in 2011.

Satchidanandan has represented India in several international literary events like the international literary festivals in Sarajevo, Berlin, Montreal, Beijing, Moscow, Ivry-sur Seine, Rotterdam, Jaipur, Delhi, Hay Festival-Trivandrum, Medellin International Poetry Festival in

Colombia, Struga Poetry Evenings in N. Macedonia, and book fairs at Delhi, Lahore, Kolkata, Abu Dhabi, Frankfurt, Leipzig, London, Paris and Moscow. He has also read and talked at Bonn, Rome, Verona, Ravenna, Leiden, NewYork, St.Petersburg, Damascus, Aberystwyth, Manchester, Dubai, Abu Dhabi, Oman, Sharjah, Singapore, Beijing, Shang Hai, Hang Zhou, Colombia, Cuba, Peru, Venezuela, Johannesburg, Skopje, Perth etc. besides most of the cities in India. Satchidanandan has been honoured with Knighthood of the Order of Merit by the Government of Italy, with the Dante Medal by the Dante Institute, Ravenna and the India-Poland Friendship Medal by the Government of Poland. He has also been an activist for secularism, environment and human rights.

www.ingramcontent.com/pod-product-compliance
Lightning Source LLC
Chambersburg PA
CBHW051731040426
42447CB00008B/1074